EXPERIMENT WITH WATER

Written by Bryan Murphy

Science Consultant: Dr. Christine Sutton
Nuclear Physics Department, University of Oxford

Education Consultant: Ruth Bessant

SCHOLASTIC INC.
New York Toronto London Auckland Sydney

First published in Great Britain in 1991 by Two-Can Publishing Ltd.

1 2 3 4 5 6 7 8 9 10   09   99 98 97 96 95 94 93 92

Photographic credits:
All photographs are copyright © Fiona Pragoff, except for the following: Cover, pp. 4, 5 (bottom right), 10, 18, 19 (top), 23 (bottom), ZEFA Picture Library (UK) Ltd.; pp. 5 (top center, top right, bottom left), 23 (top), Science Photo Library; p. 8, Oxford Scientific Films; pp. 8 (inset), 9 (center), Frank Lane Picture Agency Ltd.; pp. 9 (top and bottom), 26, 27 (center), Ardea; pp. 12, 21, 27 (top), Bruce Coleman Ltd.

All illustrations by Sally Kindberg.

CONTENTS

WATER ALL AROUND US

Water, water, water. All day long, wherever we live, we use water in many ways. Have you ever stopped and thought about it? Here are some interesting water facts.

◀ Water is the only substance on Earth that is present in three different forms—as a **liquid**, a **solid** (ice), and a **gas** (water **vapor** or **steam**).

▶ When water **boils**, it turns to **steam**.

▼ When things burn, they give off steam.

▼ People are almost 65 percent water! Tomatoes are 95 percent water.

THE WATER CYCLE

water condenses

rain

streams

rivers

water evaporates

oceans

Most of the water on Earth is in the huge, salty seas and oceans. Some of it is frozen in ice. Some of it is in lakes and rivers, or high above us in the **clouds**. And some of it is in every living thing.

Have you noticed that water is hardly ever still? Every drop of water travels on a long journey, called the **water cycle**.

You can see parts of the water cycle in your home.

◀ Pour a little water onto a plate. Leave it on a windowsill or shelf. In a few days, you can see that the level has gone down. Where do you think the water has gone? **Energy** from heat in the air has caused it to **evaporate**, or turned it into a gas called water vapor. This vapor is now part of the air you breathe. What happens next?

When air cools, it can hold less water vapor. The vapor **condenses** into a cloud of droplets.

▼ On a cold day, the warm water vapor in a bathroom condenses into liquid water on the cool mirror, and drops of water dribble down the glass like rain.

WATER AND THE WEATHER

After water vapor in the air has condensed into a cloud, it can keep changing into another form. The water droplets in a cloud move around all the time.

▶ When they bump into each other, the droplets combine into bigger droplets. When the droplets become so big and heavy the air can no longer hold them up, they fall as rain.

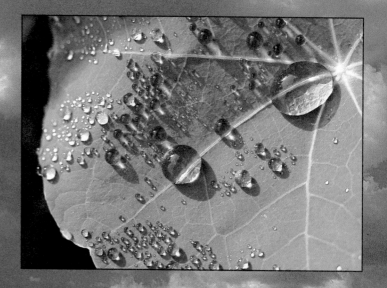

▶ If air has a lot of water vapor in it and is cooled, the vapor condenses into a cloud. If the cloud is at ground level, it is called **fog**.

◀ Sometimes it is very cold in a cloud, less than 32° Fahrenheit (0° centigrade). At this temperature, the water in a cloud freezes into tiny crystals of ice. The crystals may join together. If the air below the cloud is also cold, the ice falls as **snow**. If the air below the cloud is warmer, the falling ice will melt into rain.

◀ The air in a cloud is always moving. If an ice crystal is swept up and down through a large cloud by strong winds, it can grow into a larger ball of ice. This is called **hail**. A hailstone the size of a melon fell on Coffeyville, Kansas, on September 3, 1970.

WATER PRESSURE

Have you ever tried to touch the bottom of a swimming pool? Sometimes when you try, you can feel the water pressing on your ears. This is because water has weight. The weight of the water in the pool is the water **pressure** that pushes on your eardrums. As you go deeper, the pressure gets greater.

Try holding your head at different angles. You can still feel the pressure of the water. The pressure pushes in all directions. If you want to try this in a swimming pool, make sure that an adult or lifeguard is nearby.

▼ When seals dive deeply, they close up their nostrils to keep out the water.

You can prove that water pressure increases in deeper water. Make three holes along the side of a plastic bottle, using the sharp point of some scissors. Scissors can cut you, too, so be careful!

Cover each hole with a finger. Ask a friend to help, because you need three hands for this. Fill the bottle with water. Quickly take your fingers away. The water will spurt from the holes. Which hole has the biggest jet of water? Why do you think this is?

MAKING A SUBMARINE

Submarines are special boats that can travel under water. They have to be strong so that the great pressure deep under the ocean does not crush them.

UNDERSEAS DEVELOPME

It is easy to make a submarine that dives and surfaces just like the real thing. You can amaze your friends by making it go up and down without touching it—just like magic!

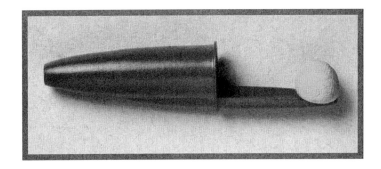

CORP.

▲ All you need is the cap of a pen, some modeling clay, and a plastic bottle with a lid that fits tightly. Weight the long, thin end of the pen cap with a small blob of clay.

▼ Put the cap in a bottle that is nearly full of water. Drop the weighted end in first. The cap should float at the surface of the water. Then screw the bottle lid on tightly.

Now for the amazing part. Ask your friends if they want the pen top to float or sink. You can control the depth of the cap by squeezing the sides of the bottle. Try it, it really works!

WEIGHT AND VOLUME

About 2,200 years ago, a king in Greece bought a crown. He was told that the crown was made of solid gold, but he wanted to be sure. The king asked a very clever man named Archimedes to check whether his new crown was made of pure gold—without harming it.

As Archimedes stepped into his bath one day, he saw the water rise around his leg. When you place an object in water, the water moves to make room for it. It rises in a container such as a bath. This told Archimedes how he could check the crown.

Things can be measured by weight and by **volume**. Archimedes thought that a crown of pure gold and a piece of pure gold of the same weight should take up the same amount of space. So he needed to compare the volume of the two.

There are easy ways to figure the volume of something shaped like a brick, using simple math. But it is very hard to figure the volume of something with an odd shape—like a crown.

Archimedes weighed the crown, and then measured out an equal weight of pure gold. He placed the crown in water and measured how much the water rose. Then he placed the pure gold in water and marked how much the water rose. The crown took up more space than the pure gold. This told Archimedes that the crown contained a different metal than gold.

Next time you take a bath, try this experiment. Before you climb in, mark the top level of the water with a small blob of toothpaste. Now get into the bath and mark the new level. Look at the difference in height between the two marks. You have just measured the volume of the parts of your body that are in the water!

Don't forget to wipe off the toothpaste marks after the experiment.

You can even measure the volume of something very exactly, just as a scientist does.

Use a cup marked to measure both cups and liters. This will make it easy to figure the volume of the solid you measure. There are different units for measuring liquids and solid materials, but one milliliter (ml) of liquid equals one cubic centimeter (cc) of anything.

Put exactly 500 ml of water into the measuring cup. Carefully put a stone into the cup and measure the new level of the water.

If the stone takes the place of 100 ml of the water, the level of the water will rise 100 ml. The volume of the stone would be 100 ml or 100 cc.

FLOATING AND SINKING

Have you ever noticed that some things float and some things sink? Make a collection of things from around the house and guess which ones will float and which ones will sink.

▲ Then fill a clear glass or plastic tank with water. Put the things in the water. Were you surprised? Did you think that the heavy things would sink and the light ones float?

Next time you go to a swimming pool, try lifting a friend in the water. You will find your friend is much lighter in water than on land.

◄ Try **submerging** something that floats, like a rubber toy. You have to push it to make it go under the surface of the water. How long does it take to rise to the surface again?

▼ Fill a balloon or clear plastic bag with water. Tell a friend that you can make it weigh nothing! Push the balloon under the water. It does not float to the top or sink to the bottom, because it contains water, and so it weighs the same as the water around it.

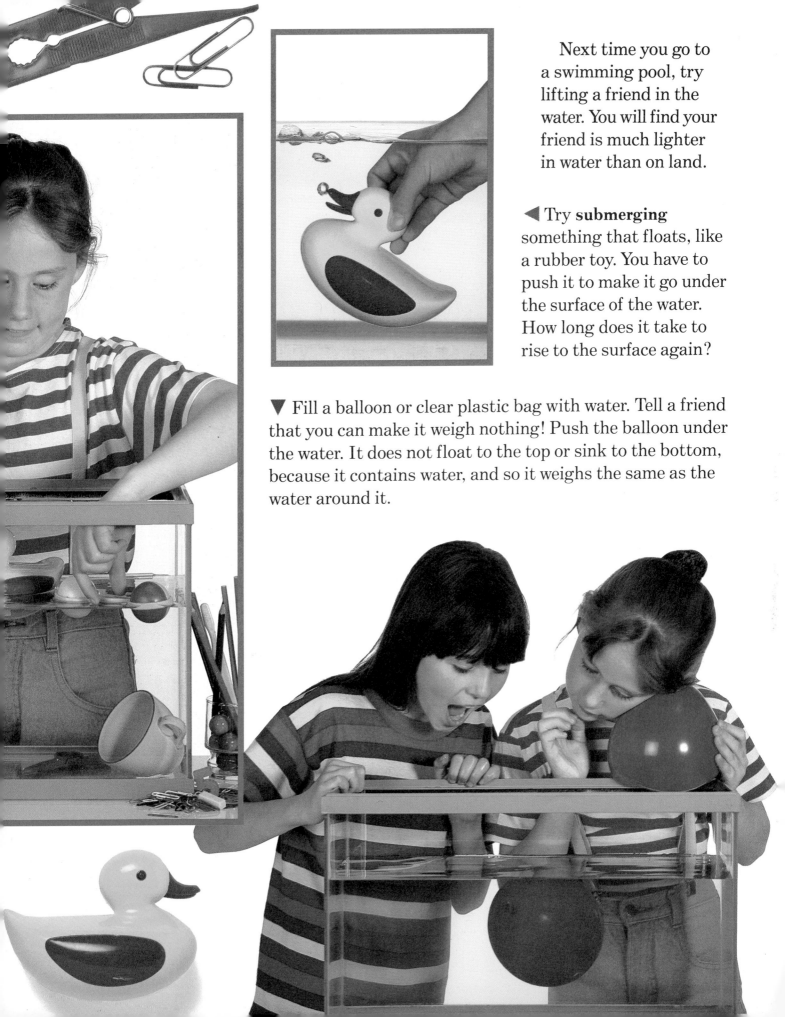

LOOKING AT SHIPS

A ship's shape and size depends on what job it is made to do. You can make different types of ships out of modeling clay. You can use a straw for a mast and paper for a sail.

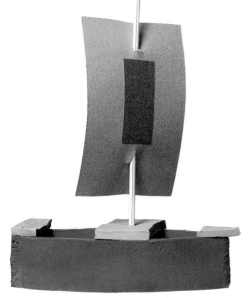

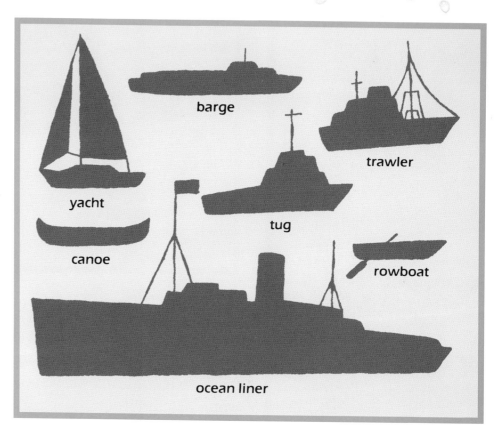

yacht

barge

trawler

tug

canoe

rowboat

ocean liner

▶ An oil tanker is a huge ship that carries oil. It has to hold a lot of oil and float in very shallow water in harbors. Look at this picture of an oil tanker. What do you notice about its shape? Is it short or long, thin or wide?

◄ A yacht is made to go very fast. That means it must be very narrow to cut quickly through the water. Try making a yacht out of modeling clay with a straw mast and a paper sail.

▼ Float your clay boat in the bathtub and blow on the sail. How can you make it go faster? See what happens if you change the shape of the sail, turn the sail to one side, or make the boat narrower.

SURFACE TENSION

Something very peculiar happens to the surface of water. You have to be very close and look very carefully to see it.

▶ Try a simple experiment. Fill a glass to the brim with water. Now put in sewing pins one at a time. You might think nothing else will fit in the glass without causing the water to spill over. But you can add a number of pins before the water spills! How many—5, 10, 20, 40? Look closely at the surface of the water as you add the pins. The water seems to be held in by an invisible skin. This force that holds the surface of a liquid together is called **surface tension**.

▶ You might be surprised to find out how strong the skin on the surface of water is. It can even support a pin!

Carefully float a small piece of paper towel on water. Quickly drop a pin on it and watch what happens when the paper sinks. The pin is left on the water's surface. If you look very closely, you should be able to see where the surface is holding it up.

Pins are very sharp, so be careful how you handle them.

▷ Some water insects, such as water
striders, use surface tension to walk on water.
Others swim just on or under the surface.
This backswimmer seems to hang suspended
from the water's surface.

BUBBLES

When dishwashing soap or detergent is added to water, it lessens the surface tension. This means that the surface will stretch farther, without breaking into water drops. You can then make **bubbles**!

▲ Gently mix about one cup (.24 liters) of dishwashing soap with five cups (1.2 l) of warm water in a bowl. To make better bubbles, add about one teaspoon (5 ml) of glycerine (you can buy glycerine at a drugstore). If the mixture does not work at once, try combining different amounts of these ingredients.

▲ You can have great fun with your bubble mixture. Ask an adult to help you make a bubble pipe by cutting four slits about one-half inch (12 ml) long in the end of a straw. Fold out the flaps. They will support the bubble as it gets bigger. Scoop up some of the bubble mixture in a cup. Dip the bubble pipe into the surface of the liquid and then blow gently.

If it is a cold day, try blowing your bubbles outside. When you fill the bubbles with your breath, you are filling them with warm air.

Which way do the bubbles go, up or down? Why do you think this is? Warm air rises and helps the bubble go up in the cold air.

◀ Look closely at a bubble. Can you see beautiful colors in it? Where have you seen colors like this before?

▼ The colors on the surface of a bubble are all the colors of the rainbow.

SEPARATING COLORS

Is black ink really black? This experiment shows you how to use water to find out. You need white coffee filter paper or paper towels, black ink (you can use a felt-tip pen or marker), a glass, a pair of scissors and, of course, water.

▶ Cut a circle out of the filter paper a bit larger than the top of the glass. Draw a small ink blot in the center. Next, make two cuts in the paper and fold the middle strip down. Carefully place the paper circle over the top of the glass so the end of the thin strip is in the water. Watch closely and you won't believe your eyes!

As the water slowly soaks up into the paper, it separates the ink into the different colors that make it up. This process is called **chromatography**, which means "color drawing." Try it with different colored inks or food coloring to see what colors they are made of.

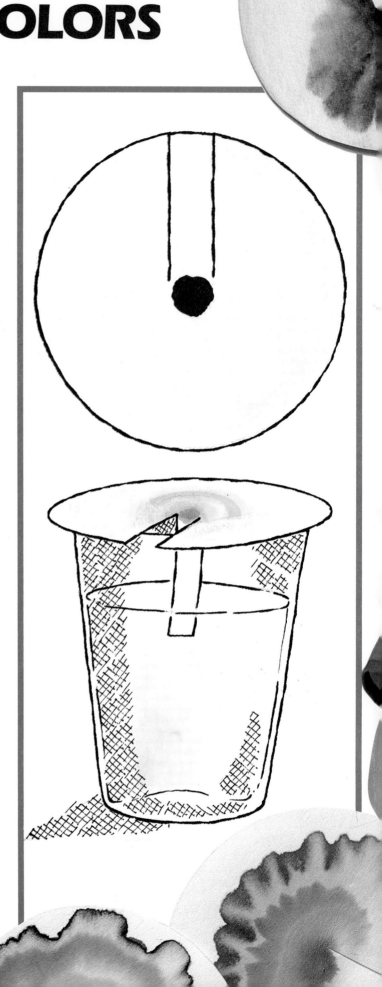

ALL-PURPOSE WATER

We use water for all sorts of things around the house: washing, drinking, watering plants. Water is also used to manufacture things. It takes 150 gallons (470 liters) of water to make the paper for one Sunday newspaper. How many other uses of water can you think of?

To be sure people will have enough water even when it does not rain, we build **dams** across rivers. A dam traps part of the flow of the river to make an artificial lake called a **reservoir**. In countries all over the world, water from reservoirs is used for drinking, manufacturing, and **irrigation**. Reservoir water can be piped to places where there is little rain. There, local farmers channel the water over their fields to their crops.

Flowing water is a source of power. Try holding your thumb over the end of a hose or faucet when water is flowing out of it. If you take your thumb away, the water will gush out.

◀ In the past, mills were sometimes powered by the force of falling water. These mills were used to grind grain into flour. The rushing water of a stream poured along a special channel and onto the blades of a huge water wheel at the side of the mill. As the wheel turned, machinery inside the mill moved huge stones to grind the grain.

◀ Nowadays the force of falling water is used to provide **electricity** for whole cities. **Hydroelectric** dams store water in reservoirs or lakes so there is a constant supply of water. Big pipes bring the water gushing downhill to hydroelectric power stations. There, the water pushes against the blades of a **turbine**, which is shaped rather like a water wheel. As the turbine spins quickly, it generates electricity.

MAKE YOUR OWN WATER WHEEL

Here is an experiment that uses the power of moving water. You will need some cardboard, an empty thread spool, a thin straw (the kind used to stir drinks), and some double-sided tape.

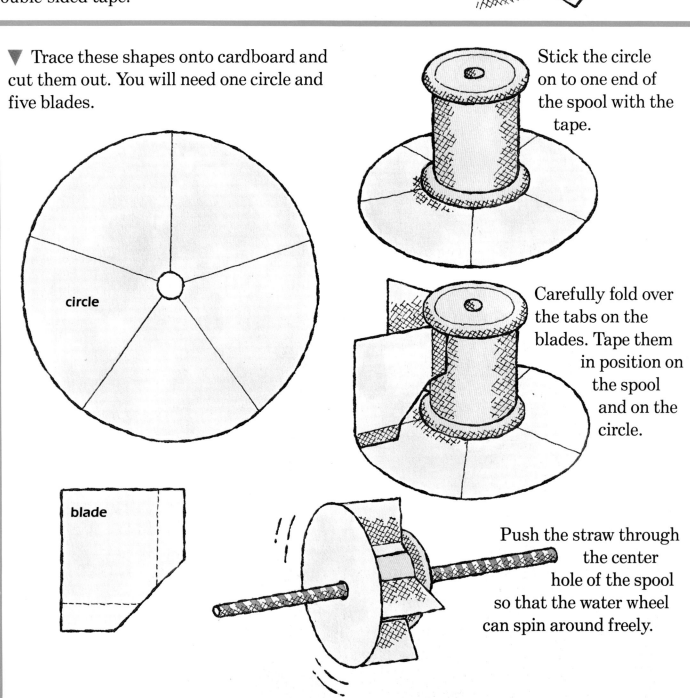

▼ Trace these shapes onto cardboard and cut them out. You will need one circle and five blades.

circle

blade

Stick the circle on to one end of the spool with the tape.

Carefully fold over the tabs on the blades. Tape them in position on the spool and on the circle.

Push the straw through the center hole of the spool so that the water wheel can spin around freely.

Try spinning the wheel in the sink under running water from the faucet. Does it spin fastest when it is up at the top, near the faucet, or farther down the stream of water? Where is the water moving fastest?

Draw some patterns on the wheel and watch it spin around.

GLOSSARY

boil: to turn a liquid into a gas by heating

bubble: a ball of gas, such as air, trapped in a liquid casing

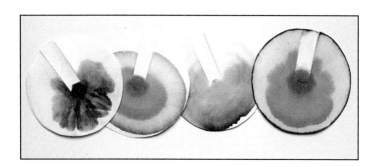

chromatography: "color drawing" by separating the chemicals within a mixture to show the different colors within it

cloud: a mass of tiny water droplets or ice crystals floating in the air

condense: to turn from gas or vapor into a liquid by cooling

dam: a blockage or wall built to hold back water

electricity: a type of energy used to make bulbs light up, turn motors, etc.

energy: power to work or be active

evaporate: to change from liquid or solid into a vapor or gas

fog: clouds near the ground

gas: a substance, such as air, that can spread out to take up all the space open to it. Gas is neither solid nor liquid.

hail: a small lump of ice that falls to the ground

hydroelectric: producing electricity by the force of water falling through turbines

liquid: a substance that flows easily. Liquid is neither gas nor solid.

pressure: the force of pushing or of weight on an area

rain: water that falls to the Earth in droplets formed from moisture in the air

reservoir: a lake, usually behind a dam, where water is stored

snow: crystals formed from water that freezes in the upper air and falls to the ground

solid: a substance that keeps its shape instead of flowing or spreading out like a liquid or gas

steam: water that has been changed into a gas or vapor by boiling

submarine: a ship that can travel underwater

submerge: to push, go, or stay underwater

surface tension: the invisible "skin" that tends to hold the surface of a liquid to the bulk of the liquid

turbine: a spinning motor that is turned by moving water or steam.

vapor: a gas or mist made of tiny drops of a substance floating in the air

volume: the space that something takes up

water cycle: the movement of water from the seas and oceans to the clouds, then to rain and rivers and back again to the seas

Index

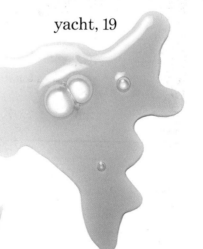